James McDermott is a playwright
East Anglia, represented by Indep
from UEA with an MA in Scrip
Royal Court Writers' Group, Soh
Hampstead Theatre's Inspire: The
He is an associate artist at HighTide and Norwich Arts Centre.

James's plays include Fast Food, which starred Jude Law (Lyric Hammersmith), Time and Tide (Park Theatre; longlisted for the Bruntwood, Papatango and Verity Bargate playwriting prizes), CAMP! (Norwich Arts Centre; UK tour), Street Life (Norwich Theatre Royal) and Rubber Ring (Pleasance Islington; UK tour). James's plays are published by Samuel French. James is currently writing new plays for Hampstead Theatre, HighTide, Eastern Angles and Norwich Playhouse. He is developing TV projects with Big Talk and Shiny Button.

James has performed his poetry at venues across the country including the Southbank Centre, Arcola Theatre and Norwich Arts Centre. He has been commissioned to write poems for The Scottish Mental Health Festival, Ian Giles's queer walking tours Open Ramble East and for Luton Culture's People Power Passion. James has also written several verse plays including Human Screens and Reveal (both commissioned and produced by Collusion). James was shortlisted for Outspoken's Prize for Poetry 2020 in the Performance Category. Manatomy is James's first poetry collection.

When James isn't writing, he teaches creative writing at Norwich Theatre Royal, Marina Theatre Lowestoft and New Wolsey Ipswich as well as in schools and colleges across East Anglia.

Follow James on Twitter @jamesliammcd and visit his website jamesmcdermottwriter.weebly.com.

Mel

MANATOMY

Best wishes & good luck with your writing!

James McDermott

[signature]

Burning Eye

Copyright © 2020 James McDermott

The author asserts the moral right under the Copyright, Designs and Patents Act 1988 to be identified as the author of this work.

All rights reserved. No part of this publication may be reproduced, stored in a retrieval system, or transmitted, in any form or by any means without the prior written consent of the author, nor be otherwise circulated in any form of binding or cover other than that in which it is published and without a similar condition being imposed on the subsequent purchaser.

This edition published by Burning Eye Books 2020

www.burningeye.co.uk

@burningeyebooks

Burning Eye Books
15 West Hill, Portishead, BS20 6LG

ISBN 978-1-911570-91-2

MANATOMY

for the friends, family and fellas who
inspired the poems in this book;
for teenage me, who didn't like himself
because he'd been shamed;
for all those people who don't yet like
themselves because they've been shamed.

CONTENTS

MAN

EPILOGUE

GRINDR PROFILE 2020

James, 26

Online now

Hello. I'm a writer and creative writing teacher. I love writing, reading, walking, laughing and deep chats. I'm not mad about the beard either but without it I look like Clare Balding so…

Height: 178cm

Weight: 9st 10lb

Body Type: Average

Position: Versatile Bottom

Ethnicity: White

Relationship Status: Single

My Tribes: Geek, Rugged, Twink

Looking For: Dates, Friends, Relationships, Right Now

Gender: Cis Man

Pronouns: He/Him/His

HIV Status: Negative

BOY

BOYS' DRESSES

24th November 1993.

Norfolk and Norwich Hospital.

Mum and Dad are about to give birth.

Well… Dad isn't; he's just holding Mum's legs in the air.

With one final push, their baby daughter enters the world.

Dad wraps her up in a towel, wraps her up in his arms…

But something's wrong…

Mum is sure I'll be a girl – she can 'feel it in her water' – so, against Dad's advice, she never asks my gender when she has a scan.

When I'm in the womb, she calls me 'my princess' and to stop me kicking, she sings me the songs of Cher.

She buys me dresses, bonnets and booties and she makes Dad paint my walls pink and plaster them in pictures of Peggy Patch from Playdays.

Even when I turn out to be a boy, Mum still wants me to wear the dresses; she hasn't kept the receipts, so she can't return them, and she can't afford to buy new baby clothes.

As Mum wears the trousers, she makes sure that until she's paid, I wear the dresses.

Even when I'm in trousers, Mum still plays me the songs of Cher and calls me her princess…

PHALLIC BOTTLES

1996.

Milk, Maryland cookies and pudding-bowl haircuts.

The day Mum has to go back to work after maternity leave.

Up until now, I've spent loads of time with Mum and very little time with Dad.

Maybe I choose to spend loads of time with Mum as female company appeals to me.

Maybe I choose to spend loads of time with Mum because I'm a baby and she's my mum.

Or maybe, as I'm three, I get no choice in which parent I spend the most time with.

Whether or not I want to, I have to accompany Mum to Now Is the Winter of Our Discount Tans, where I listen to Mum and her mates talk about men.

Whilst I'm always at Mum's side, I'm never at her breast as she won't breastfeed.

Instead of growing up sucking on a woman's tit I grow up sucking on a phallic bottle…

Unlike other little boys I'm never dependent on or desperate for the breast.

When Mum goes back to work after maternity leave, every day she drops me off at nursery.

And I hate it.

I don't connect with the boys who play football and soldiers.

Nursery won't let me connect with the girls who play mums and princesses.

I feel so lonely.

I feel like it's Mum's fault.

I feel like the first woman I love hurts and abandons me…

As Dad finishes work before Mum does, every afternoon Dad rescues me from nursery.

And I love him for that.

We grow closer because of that.

The first man I love seems to save me and love me back…

When me and Dad wait for Mum to come home, we finally get to spend time together and he finally gets to introduce me to his man's world.

But it isn't a world of sports and sports cars; my dad hates sport and he drives a Daewoo Matiz.

My dad is a painter and decorator, and so in my formative years I never get exposed to a conventionally masculine world.

Instead, Dad introduces me to a world of artistic expression: paint, colour, fun felt, smelly gel pens and glitter!

SPICE GIRLS DOLLS

1998.

Happy Meals, TY Beanie Babies and Tots TV.

A Saturday afternoon in Toys 'R' Us.

Mum and Dad say I can pick any gift I want to celebrate my first full week at school.

I could have a toy Budgie the Little Helicopter or a remote-controlled Brum.

But I don't want either of those things.

I want a Posh Spice doll.

Dad suggests a Tamagotchi.

Mum tells Dad that a Tamagotchi won't spice up my life.

Dad tells Mum that she's not to buy me a girl's doll. Gay boys play with dolls.

And this is the first time I hear that word.

I don't know what it means, but I know it can't mean something nice because of the way Dad spits it out of his mouth.

Whilst I don't know what that word means, my ears burn when I hear it.

Like Mum said ears are supposed to when someone is talking about you...

So I ask Dad what it means.

Dad tells me that it, um... it means happy, son-bun...

I ask him if he's gay, then.

He says no. I'm not gay. I'm married to your mother…

I know being gay doesn't mean being happy.

Why would Dad be this angry about me being a happy boy?

Whatever nasty thing it really means, I realise it has something to do with dolls.

I only want a Posh Spice doll as I want to see what's under her dress.

I only want a Posh Spice doll as I love the Spice Girls and want all the merchandise.

But then and there I vow that I'll try to stop playing with dolls.

Then Dad won't be angry.

Then I won't be a gay boy.

I think I've still got that Tamagotchi…

ALL WILLIES GREAT AND SMALL

1999.

Wax crayons, PVA glue, Biff and Chip and The Magic Key.

Class 2B.

I'm sat at the blue table with my best mate Adam.

Miss Benton, a woman who looks like Auntie Mabel from *Come Outside*, is trying to teach my class the words to 'All Creatures Great and Small'.

But I'm far more interested in the small creature that's peeping out of Adam's shorts.

I look him in the eye.

He looks me in the eye.

Like Biff and Chip, me and Adam do everything together.

But when Adam wants us to sit together with our willies out...

I don't think so.

But when Adam says if I don't get mine out he won't play out tonight...

He stares at mine.

I stare at his.

The first genitals I see other than mine...

And the more I stare at his, the more I start to want to touch his...

Adam snaps at me: what you doing?

Adam says his dad says you're gay if you like playing with boys' willies.

I snap back that my dad says you're gay if you play with dolls and aren't married to my mum.

I look him in the eye.

He looks me in the eye.

Then Adam shrugs, grabs my willy, I grab his and we toy with each other as if we're Play-Doh.

The first genitals I touch other than mine…

I know Dad was lying when he said being gay means being happy, so is Adam's dad right?

Are you gay if you like playing with boys' willies?

Because I like playing with Adam's…

Maybe that's just because I'm seven and I like playing with everything.

But playing with Lego doesn't make my blood catch fire and my skin tingle…

I'm still toying with Adam when Miss Benton starts singing the next hymn:

'He's Got the Whole World in His Hands'.

SOME MOTHERS DO 'AVE 'EM

2003.

Frank Lampard, *Yu-Gi-Oh!* and the Fast Food Song.

B*Witched have just split up, so I'm on the lookout for a new obsession.

One Sunday afternoon, I'm channel surfing and I find it…

Other boys want Burberry baseball caps. I want a beret.

Other boys want toy tanks. I want a tank top.

Other boys want to be Frank Lampard. I want to be Frank Spencer.

Aged ten, I am obsessed with the 1970s BBC sitcom *Some Mothers Do 'Ave 'Em.*

Dad taught me how to talk and so I talk like Dad.

But one day, my voice decides to start talking like Frank Spencer.

Dad asks me why I'm speaking like that camp twat.

I tell him it's because he's got the funniest voice ever, Dad. Maybe speaking like him will make me just as funny. And what does *camp* mean?

Dad says camp means… acting as if you're gay.

I say back, but Frank's not gay. He's married to Ooh Betty. He doesn't like touching boys' willies or playing with dolls.

Dad says, but he acts like he does. You speak like Frank if you like doing that. You don't wanna speak like you're funny, do you, buggerlugs?

I say, ooh, no, Dad… I mean no, Dad. Of course I don't wanna speak like that.

To stop Dad being angry at me, I try to speak how Dad taught me to speak.

But I can't.

My old voice feels like an impression I can't quite do any more.

The impression I can't stop doing now feels like my own voice.

CHANGING ROOM

2005.

Sweat, socks and Lynx.

The boys' changing rooms.

In here, I become familiar with boys' naked bodies long before it's even legal for me to become familiar with girls' naked bodies.

During the most sexually formative years of my life, school makes me rugby-tackle boys, then wash my tackle with boys.

One PE lesson, I trip over my PE bag.

And the bear pit erupts with cheers and jeers and I know what's coming next because he does it to everyone who falls over…

Shirtless, Manny wraps his arm round my head and gives me a monkey scrub.

And as my baby face touches his man's body…

He gives me a hard-on.

After that, I fall over in every PE lesson.

And in every PE lesson, Manny gets me in a headlock and I get a stiffy.

And every time I do, I feel amazing, appalling, alive and ill.

I get a hard-on because of a boy's touch…

Maybe I instinctively get a hard-on when a boy touches me because I was born gay.

Maybe I get a hard-on because I'm eleven and I'd get hard if anyone touched me.

Or maybe I become used to – and used to being aroused by – a boy's touch before I can touch a girl, trick myself into thinking I must be gay, stop pursuing girls, start pursuing boys and gradually make myself gay…

TRICK OR TREAT

31st October 2006.

Eve's Halloween party.

As a goth I should be having a scream tonight, but everyone bar me is getting drunk, getting off and getting down to 'Thriller'.

I head out onto the crazy paving to self-harm with the pin of my Morrissey badge.

But I decide not to as I don't want to get blood on my cloak; it's vintage.

I'm just about to leave the party when Eve appears out of nowhere.

Eve drains her hooch, puts her hands on my hips and pulls me close.

Then she gives me a pelvic thrust that drives me up against the trellis.

This is it.

She wants to get off.

She wants to get down.

And so do I…

Because every boy in my year except me has kissed a girl.

And every boy in my year says if you haven't kissed a girl yet then you're probably…

Well, I'm gonna prove them wrong.

I'm gonna kiss a girl.

I'm gonna show them that I'm not—

Suddenly she's on me, her tongue is in me.

And it's horrible.

Because her lips are that big and wet, it's like kissing an armband.

Because she tastes of hooch and stinks of Frizz-Ease.

And because as she's kissing me…

As she's kissing me, all I can think is I wish Manny was doing this.

Suddenly Eve grabs my hand, stuffs it under her top and inside her bra.

I'm a thirteen-year-old boy and my hand is holding a breast…

And my body feels nothing.

My body doesn't know what to do.

My head tells my body it should feel something now.

My head begs my body to do something now.

But it won't.

Or it can't.

Maybe my body doesn't really fancy Eve and my head isn't really in the moment.

Because my head is thinking…

I'm disappointed this chest isn't flat and toned.

I'm disappointed this chest isn't hairy.

Maybe my body is used to playing with my own flat hairy chest.

Or maybe I was born gay and so I instinctively expect to feel a man's body.

I wriggle my hand out from under Eve's top.

Inside the next song starts up; it's Michael Jackson's 'She's Out of My Life'.

THE PRINCE OF MINCE

2006.

The Scissor Sisters, the Tenth Doctor and Julian Clary.

I first see this makeup-wearing stand-up on *Live at the Apollo*.

And he walks like no man I have ever seen.

Dad taught me how to walk and so I walk like Dad.

But the more I watch Julian walking like that, the more I want to walk like him.

Because I'm an impressionable teenager who imitates everything.

And because seeing that walk feels like it unlocks something in me.

So when I walk, I start wiggling my hips and sticking my hands out and I love it.

Because something as commonplace as walking now feels as fun as dancing.

Because now heads turn as I turn and people stop in their tracks as I walk in mine.

Because walking like this feels right.

Dad asks me what I'm mincing about like a gay boy for.

When he called me that before, I stopped playing with dolls.

But when he calls me that now…

I don't stop mincing.

The more he protests, the more I mince.

My mince becomes a march against him.

But I don't keep mincing just to defy Dad.

I don't stop because I can't stop.

I try to walk how Dad taught me to again, but it feels uncomfortable.

Like I'm walking in shoes that aren't mine.

Like I'm walking in shoes I've grown out of.

SPILLING THE BEANS

2007.

Mika, *Shameless* and Elliott Tittensor.

And the year every boy I know starts to… you know?

At lunchtimes, we aren't playing with Beyblades and Tech Decks any more.

We're all queuing up for the disabled toilet to play with ourselves.

When we aren't doing it, we trade tips and tales about doing it.

I tell my mates I've been doing it over all the fit girls in Year Eleven.

Of course this is… well, a pile of wank.

Because I've been doing it over my mates.

I don't want to.

I try not to.

I try to do it over Eve and her gorgeous graduated bob or Gen in her cracking Top Shop top, but my body won't let me; my dick stays as small as a Tic Tac.

Then I imagine Adam jerking off or Manny jerking me off and it's up like a Pringles tube.

All right: a Smarties tube…

Afterwards I'm up all night because I know what this means.

But.

It could be a phase.

And when I wank I might just imagine my mates wanking because I'm so used to hearing them talk about wanking.

And I am yet to… spill my beans.

If I haven't done that over boys, I don't need to read *The Ballad of Reading Gaol* just yet.

But then, one night, as I'm flicking through late-night telly…

I see him.

Elliott Tittensor, AKA Carl Gallagher in Channel 4's *Shameless*.

I tune in every week praying that he has a scene.

If he does, I film it on my phone and watch it back until I'm out of battery.

My head tells me this is because he's a really good actor actually, but my body knows otherwise.

Sometimes I get lucky and he has a sex scene.

My head tells me I'm interested in seeing the naked women he has sex with actually, but my body knows otherwise.

One week I am blessed: in one sex scene, I get to see his come face.

I record it and jerk off to it again and again, and then, on Wednesday 23rd May 2007…

I spill my beans.

I don't sleep for weeks.

Because of realisation.

Guilt.

Terror.

Because I'm up every night reading Wilde.

And because I can't stop wanking…

SUCKING COCK AND BEING BUMMED

2010.

Sweat, socks and Lynx.

I'm alone in the changing rooms after Scottish country dancing club when I trip over my sporran.

There's a cheer from the doorway; it's Manny.

He's just had after-school football club.

And suddenly he has me in a headlock, he monkey-scrubs my head, he presses his…

Presses his package into my thigh.

He pulls me into the showers and I pull him in for a kiss.

But he pushes me away and pushes me to my knees.

And with a dig and a wriggle he pulls down his shorts, his boxers and…

There it is.

Here it is.

But what now?

I've had classes on handling a cucumber but not on handling a cock.

Do I kiss it?

Do I lick it?

My head and my body tell me I want to do something with it.

Well, I do until it flushes and rushes to its full size, then stands there enlarged and charged and winking at me...

Then I realise just how massive this is.

The moment, not the penis.

Although that's pretty mass—

There is a penis in my mouth.

There is a penis.

In my mouth.

And suddenly...

Suddenly I know exactly what to do with it.

It's like I was born to do it.

And doing it makes me feel amazing, appalling, alive and ill.

Suddenly Manny is pulling out my mouth, pulling me to my feet.

My body moves in for a kiss, my hand pulls his hand to my crotch, but he pushes me away, spins me round.

And suddenly my hands are pulling down my boxers even though my head is saying *no, don't do this, you're straight.*

And my body is bending over even though my head is saying *no, don't do this, you're straight.*

And then I feel a hot wet bullet of spit hit my hole and suddenly my head and my body tell me I want this.

And Manny's hands grab my cheeks and my head and my body tell me this is right.

And Manny's hands part my cheeks and my head and my body—

OW OW OW IT'S HORRIBLE GET IT OUT GET IT OUT.

Manny pulls it out.

He asks if I'm okay.

And… I am okay.

I'm okay because gay sex was horrible.

I'm okay because I'm not gay!

But my body didn't know what to do when Eve wanted sex with me…

And my body instinctively knew what to do when Manny wanted sex with me…

And my head and my body told me that I wanted sex with Manny…

Yeah, but if I didn't like sex with Manny then I mustn't be gay, right?

Then Manny asks if he can try again.

And I don't know why, but my mouth says he's more than welcome to try while my head says *no, mate, because I'm not gay*…

And it's agony as he forces his way in, it's horrible once he's found his way in because I'm straight.

I realise in that moment that everyone's been wrong all these years. I mustn't be gay if gay sex makes me feel so—

Oooh.

Oooh, that's nice.

Shit.

And as Manny has his way with me I feel amazing, appalling, alive and ill.

Then suddenly it's all over.

Manny shoots his juice, calls me queer and he's gone.

I mop up his mess with my sporran.

And that's it.

That's? It?

Those two minutes were what I've lost nights pulling myself off over, years dreaming over, youth fretting over?

He wouldn't even kiss me.

And he called me queer.

Which suggests that he isn't.

Having done that, either we both are or we both aren't, right?

But if I enjoyed sucking cock and being bummed, surely that means I am just a little bit queer?

Or maybe that means that sucking cock and being bummed are just something I liked doing today, something I liked trying today but something I might never want to do again?

THE HAPPY CAMPER

2010.

Books, books, books.

I'm sixteen when my media teacher gives me Rupert Everett's autobiography.

I give her an arched eyebrow in return because books do not do it for me.

Maybe this is because every book I have to read at school only ends happily ever after if the boy gets the girl.

Maybe this is because every book I have to read at school contains no gay characters and so I grow up feeling like a ghost no one believes in.

The books my teachers made me read made me stop reading.

But I cannot stop reading this one book this one teacher makes me read.

Maybe this is just because it's well-written and witty and engaging.

Maybe I tell myself I love it because my media teacher told me I'd love it and, as I love my media teacher, I don't want to let her down.

Or maybe I love this story of a gay writer-performer's life because it speaks to me, even if I'm not yet sure what it's saying or who 'me' is.

After reading this book, I want to read more, and so my media teacher introduces me to the work of Armistead Maupin and Alan Bennett, Harvey Fierstein and Jonathan Harvey.

During one of the most impressionable times of my life, the only texts I read are gay.

Before reading these books, I feel like an alien.

No one else has ever touched a boy's willy in class, sucked a boy's willy in the changing rooms or imagined kissing a boy when they're about to kiss a girl.

Reading these books makes me realise that other people have experienced these things.

Reading these books makes me realise that, like their authors, I am not an alien.

But reading the words of these authors isn't enough; I want to start speaking, acting and dressing like my favourite writers.

Dad taught me how to get dressed, so I always dress like Dad.

But suddenly I'm wearing paisley shirts, corduroy trousers and pepperpot brogues.

I'm quoting Wilde and wearing a carnation in my school blazer buttonhole.

I'm trying to speak like Stephen Fry.

Dad said that camp means acting as if you're gay.

Dad was wrong.

Suddenly I learn that real camp means acting *as if*.

As if I'm a gay novelist.

As if I'm the wittiest person in the world.

As if names could never bruise me.

If anyone spits insults at me for being a weak, effeminate poser, I spit quotes back at them and feel stronger, more masculine and more real than I've ever felt before.

I wear my camp as if it's armour.

Words and wit become my weapons to silence everyone.

Except Dad.

Dad asks me why I'm dressing and talking like that. Gays dress and talk like that.

To placate Dad, I do try to stop dressing like this and dress how Dad taught me to dress.

But I can't.

It feels uncomfortable.

It feels like I'm wearing a costume I've grown out of.

WRITE ME POEMS ON POST-ITS

2011.

The first school assembly on the first day of sixth form.

We're singing 'All Creatures Great and Small' when a great creature I think I recognise sneaks into the hall.

Our eyes meet over a sea of blazers.

And I see my past and my future in those eyes...

Adam!

It's his first day at my school and when I see him again, I feel like it's my first day too.

We spend breaktimes, lunchtimes and night-times together.

We talk on Bebo, Myspace and MSN and soon enough we're...

Best friends again...

We tell each other everything.

He tells me everything about his new girlfriend.

Eve...

But I don't tell him how I start to feel about him.

I don't tell him he makes my insides warm, my outsides tingle and my whole body smile.

I don't tell him I want us to go for walks and talks and drives and dates and dinners.

I don't tell him I want to be in his bed, his head, his heart, his hands, his pants and his plans.

I don't tell him I want him to visit on birthdays with books I loved and lost as a boy and mentioned just once in casual conversation.

I don't tell him I want us to buy a flat and flatpacks for our single room with our double bed.

I don't tell him I want us to mix up our bodies, our books, our laundry and our lives.

I don't tell him I want us to buy baby clothes, school shoes and graduation photos.

I don't tell him I want him to make me mixtapes.

I don't tell him I want him to give me a nickname.

I don't tell him I want him to write me poems on Post-its.

I don't tell him I want him to text me first sometimes.

I don't tell him I think he might be the answer to something.

I don't tell him I think he might be a great big question I want to spend my life trying to answer.

I don't tell him I think he might be the missing piece to my puzzle.

But I tell myself that the hunger with which I want to tell him…

The agony I feel at not being able to tell him…

The hell I feel at not being able to have him…

I tell myself that this probably means that…

I love him.

I love a boy…

The first person I fall for is a fella.

I've never felt like this about a girl.

But I've never felt like this about any other boy…

Maybe I love this boy and not boys, then.

Maybe loving this one boy leads me to love other boys.

Maybe loving this boy before I love a girl leads me to think I must be gay, so I stop pursuing girls, start pursuing boys and gradually make myself gay.

TRUE COLOURS

2012.

I'm Facebook-stalking Adam as I listen to Eva Cassidy sing 'Hallelujah, I Love Him So'.

I'm just about to harmonise with her when I clock Dad standing in my doorway.

Dad says he just wants to bring me this prezzy to celebrate me getting an offer from uni.

It's an action figure of the Rock, my favourite WWE wrestler.

I've been a fan since I saw him on telly fighting with Randy Orton.

Since I've been a fan of wrestling, Dad's been a fan of mine.

Mum appears in the doorway and says, ooh, so he's allowed a doll now, then, is he?

Dad tells Mum that this isn't a doll; this is an action figure.

Mum tells Dad it's an action figure of a muscly man in just his pants.

Dad looks at Mum…

At the Rock…

At me…

At my posters of Randy Orton kissing his muscles…

At the Facebook photos of Adam on my laptop screen…

And as Dad looks back at me…

Eva Cassidy's next song starts up.

She sings something about seeing my true colours.

And Dad…

Dad laughs a laugh that's a lid on a cry.

Then Dad cuddles me.

Then Mum joins the hug, and through tears they tell me they love me and that they've always known who I am, and I stand there in the middle of it wondering, if they've always known who I am, then why don't I know yet?

Because I didn't like what I did with Manny.

And I don't like how loving Adam makes me feel.

I haven't even kissed a boy yet…

I'VE GOT THE WHOLE WORLD IN MY HANDS

2012.

Results day.

Adam's come round for Prosecco, party rings and caterpillar cake.

I got three A's!

Adam gets three C's.

He says he doesn't know what Eve got, he doesn't care, the two-timer can go to hell.

Eve's started seeing Manny.

I tell Adam not to worry as I can't see that lasting.

And Adam tells me that if today is goodbye then he just wants me to know that he loves me.

I tell him that I, um… I love him too. Madly. I have for years.

He tells me that he, um… meant as a mate…

I say oh… no, yeah, no, yeah, no, I know, me too, me too…

And then he kisses me.

And because I've always done what Adam's done…

I kiss him back.

And I feel like Sleeping Beauty waking up after eighteen years.

And I feel something inside me lock.

And I feel something inside me unlock.

And when I hold him to kiss him again…

I feel like I've got the whole world in my hands.

YOUTH

TIME LORD

I was eleven when I knew.
I wanted to be Doctor Who.

I wanted time to go backwards.
I wanted time to go forwards.

I was made small and blue outside.
I felt bigger on the inside.

I looked like a human, but
I felt alien underneath.

I felt like a stoic loner
who could not let humans get close.

Humans said I could not love, but
I had two hearts and twice their love.

I wanted to regenerate
into someone Dad would not hate.

ADDRESSED

And then she walked in
on me in her dress,
stood before her dead
mum's mirror, my eyes
black and blue, lips red,
she started sobbing,
told me it's not that
she hates me like this;
she is scared of
what Dad would do if
I am found like this.

THE GAY LORD'S PRAYER

Our fathers in childhood,
hallowed be your names,
show us your emotions,
never stop cuddling us
and teach us that being a man is about being brave enough to
be your own man.
Give us every day your love and respect.
Forgive your generation's sins
of teaching you homophobia and toxic masculinity
and lead us not into toxic relationships
but show us from birth that it is not sinful but natural
to have a loving, demonstrative relationship with a man.
Now and forever,
amen.

HERO

Mum looks eighteen-year-old me in the eyes and I tell her that I am gay.

And for a second she looks at me with eyes that aren't a mother's.

She looks at me with her dad's eyes.

She looks at me with eyes full of homophobic abuse, anal sex and AIDS.

Then she looks away.

And she looks at a framed photo of me aged five dressed as Baby Spice, laughing and loving life.

She looks at a framed photo of me aged thirteen dressed as Oscar Wilde for World Book Day, laughing and loving life.

She looks at a framed photo of me aged eighteen with my arms around the shoulders of my best friend Lyndon, laughing and loving life.

Then she looks back at me, eighteen, crying and hating life because I need to know she still loves me.

And then Mum looks at me with mother's eyes again, eyes full of love and fear, and she hugs me.

A few days later I get home from school and I find on my bed an Oscar Wilde book I don't already have.

Inside the book Mum has written, *I love you. Live your life. Be brave enough to be yourself.*

*

Mum looks her husband of twenty-five years in the eyes when he asks for his monthly £200 allowance.

And Mum looks at her husband with eyes that aren't a lover's.

She looks at her husband with eyes that say, *I am sick of keeping you.*

She looks at her husband with eyes that say, *Why did I settle for a man who left school at twelve, who can hardly read or write, has no social skills and so is completely unemployable?*

She looks at her husband with eyes that say, *Why have you never tried to address those issues in the twenty-five years we've been together?*

But then Mum looks at her husband's eyes.

And in them she sees him twenty-five years ago.

She sees a man who was happy with his job on a caravan site, who never wanted a wife or kids.

She sees a man who had to leave the job he loved to become a house-husband as his job didn't pay enough, whereas Mum's job did.

She sees a man who spends his monthly £200 allowance on her, their house and their sons, and doing that helps him forget that he left school at twelve and is unemployable.

And she looks at him with lover's eyes again.

And she gives him the £200.

*

Mum looks my twenty-year-old brother in the eyes, and he tells her he doesn't want to join the police any more because he and his girlfriend of two months are pregnant and they're keeping the baby.

And she looks at him with eyes that aren't a mother's.

She looks at him with the eyes of someone who was going to become a writer but who became a mum instead.

She looks at him with the eyes of someone who, to make ends meet, ended up working in the health service and hated every minute of it.

She looks at him with the eyes of someone who still works in the health service, still hates every minute of it, but stands it to support one son who wants to be a writer and another son who wants to be a policeman.

Then, on the wall, she clocks a framed photo of him twenty years ago, newborn and precious.

A framed photo of him fifteen years ago, all milk teeth and blue eyes and pudding-bowl haircut.

A framed photo of him ten years ago, all muddy knees and hair gel and playing policemen.

A framed photo of him five years ago, all cheekbones and shoe polish and police cadet uniform.

And Mum looks back at my brother with mother's eyes again, and then she hugs him.

And the next time my brother visits, there's a Moonpig card waiting for him.

On the front of the card is a photo of my brother in his police cadet uniform.

Inside the card Mum's written, *Congrats, son. I'll never give up on you. Never give up on your dreams.*

*

Mum looks her ninety-year-old mother in the eyes when, on Christmas Day, her mother gets up off the sofa and a shit falls from her nightie and onto Mum's new carpet.

And Mum screams at her mother.

And Mum looks at her mother with eyes that aren't a daughter's.

She looks at her with eyes that still remember a mother who stood by and watched a father hit and spit and shout at her daughter.

She looks at her with eyes that still remember a mother who would deliberately embarrass her in front of boyfriends.

She looks at her with eyes that still remember a mother who would try to break up her daughter's marriage because she didn't like her daughter's husband.

But then Mum looks at her mother's eyes.

And in them my Mum sees her mother being hit and spat at by her husband.

She sees her mother being embarrassed by her husband in front of his friends.

She sees her mother perpetually unhappy because of marriage.

And Mum apologises for shouting at her mother.

And Mum picks up a piece of Christmas paper and she uses it to pick up her mother's shit.

*

Mum looks into the eyes of a stranger in the street who has just taken the piss out of her for dressing in 1940s clothes.

My Mum goes out shopping and socialising every weekend dressed in vintage clothes and makeup.

She always looks like a cross between a forties housewife and a little girl.

And Mum looks into the eyes of the stranger who's stopped her .

And Mum tells the stranger to live their life and be brave enough to be themselves.

And then my Mum keeps on going.

I WAS RAISED ON JAMES BOND FILMS

I was raised on James Bond films.
Connery taught me
men drink a lot;
men don't cry;
men have lots of sex;
men fight;
men slap women on the arse.

I was raised on James Bond films.
Lazenby taught me
men get married;
men don't cry;
men have their voices dubbed;
men fight;
men lose their wives.

I was raised on James Bond films.
Moore taught me
men wear suits;
men don't cry;
men hide emotions behind humour;
men fight;
men should not wear flares.

I was raised on James Bond films.
Dalton taught me
men bear grudges;
men don't cry;
men don't have friendships;
men fight;
men don't stick around.

I was raised on James Bond films.
Brosnan taught me
men gamble;
men don't cry;
men live to work and win;

men fight;
men only see women as conquests or rivals.

I was raised on James Bond films.
Craig taught me
men are muscly;
men don't cry;
men get hurt if they fall in love;
men fight;
men need to look good in Speedos.

I was raised on James Bond films.

FOOTBALL IS SO GAY

An old coach teaches
fit young men how to
penetrate the goals
of other young men
and how to protect
their own goals from
being penetrated.
If they shoot and score and
thrash the other boys
they win the cock-
shaped trophy and
get to hug and kiss
before showering
naked together.

TEACHING KIDS ABOUT GAY RELATIONSHIPS

Teaching kids about gay relationships
will not make kids have gay relationships.
Teaching me about straight relationships
did not make me have straight relationships,
just as teaching me about menstruation
did not make me start having periods,
just as teaching me about religion
did not make me believe in religion,
just as teaching me geography
did not make me become a rainforest,
just as teaching me French, Spanish, German
did not make me French, Spanish or German,
just as teaching me my country's history
did not make me invade and colonise.

But being taught language and history,
science, religion and geography
helped me to see the world's complexity,
helped me to see the world's diversity,
helped me to see the world's bigger than me,
my classroom, my town and my family.
This helped me to develop empathy
with anyone who's not the same as me
so when I had to leave my family,
my classroom, school, town, county and country
I had been taught by teachers how to be
an adult in the twenty-first century.

THANKS TO ALL MY STRAIGHT MATES

Thanks to all my straight mates
who didn't treat me differently,
who didn't stop talking to me,
who didn't just talk about my sexuality
but who would talk about my sexuality
when I needed someone to talk with me.

Thanks to all my straight mates
who didn't use my body as a punchbag,
who didn't use my name as a punchline,
who saved me a place in the lunch line,
who knew who I was before I did and didn't mind.

Thanks to all my straight mates
who in our cruel school
risked becoming so uncool
by shouting down those hurtful fools
with *shut up, you stupid tools.*

Thanks to all my straight mates
who still changed next to me in PE,
who still stood next to me to pee,
who let me see what I needed to see
and so let me learn about me and my homosexuality.

Thanks to all my straight mates
who still invited me to parties,
who kissed me pissed at parties,
who danced with me at parties,
who didn't do this out of pity,
who didn't do this to laugh at me
but who did this for a laugh with me,
who did this because they loved me.

Thanks to all my straight mates
who have stayed my straight mates,
who have now just become my mates,

who come with me to gay clubs,
who drink with me in straight pubs,
who come see every gay play,
who are always asked if they're gay.
I just want to say
thanks
to all my straight mates.

NORFOLK LIVING

Life is never as bright as the lights from the fruity;
time moves as slowly as tractors drive in the country
and the days are as grey as the fish from the chippy,
afternoons are as flat as the hills in this county
and nights as dead as the high street in Wells-next-the-Sea.
Bingo is the only place to go to get lucky,
the pubs are as empty as second homes in Blakeney
and the only clubs are dominoes, boules and rummy.
(And the only cock round here crows at five thirty.)
Whilst, unlike buses, bigotry comes regularly,
and it's only on postcards that Norfolk is sunny,
and the only change here's in pots for charity,
this silly little county is home sweet home to me.

WANTING

I wanted Harry
to show me his
muscles I wanted
Jake to let me play
with his cock I want-
ed to play husbands
and wives I wanted
Kane to show me up
his shorts I wanted
Dan to let me be
his girl I wanted
Sam to show me how
he comes I want some
boy who wants me too

EXT. HIGH STREET, NORWICH CITY CENTRE – DAY

EXT. HIGH STREET, NORWICH CITY CENTRE — DAY

5pm.

A sea of shoes, suits, swinging hands.

The speed and the noise of the high street at rush hour.

And in the middle of the crowd...

Not slow motion but the feel of slow motion as —

Two hands, strangers' hands, men's hands, knock into each other.

Silence now, like a shock, the sounds of the city muted.

Just the sound of these strangers' hands brushing over each other.

Pull back, revealing the two strangers who have stopped in the crowd.

JAMES, 18, cute, clumsy, earphones in, smiles an apology at —

LYNDON, 18, cool, sexy, who doesn't smile back.

Hold the silence...

The stare...

Then Lyndon grins!

James takes out his earphones.

The music he's listening to floods the scene.

And Lyndon's grin grows wider, like a door, opening...

As James blinks —

SMASH CUT into:

INT. HALLWAY, JAMES'S FLAT — NIGHT

James and Lyndon burst through the front door, snogging, hard.

Lyndon pushing James up against the wall —

James's hands in Lyndon's hair —

Lyndon's hands tugging at James's clothes.

Music continues over all this.

INT. BEDROOM, JAMES'S FLAT — NIGHT

Lyndon and James on the bed, James on his back, Lyndon on top, facing each other.

Lyndon shagging James.

Slow, sensual, intimate.

Lyndon kisses James's lips.

His nose.
His eyelids.

Then Lyndon rests his forehead on James's.

They stare into each other.

The stillness...

The intimacy...

Then they both burst out laughing!

James sticks his tongue out, licks the tip of
Lyndon's nose.

Lyndon nibbles the tip of James's tongue.

Still laughing, they kiss, both so happy.

JUMP CUT to James and Lyndon dancing to the
music on James's bed, hands in the air, in just
their boxers, loving life!

James holds out his hands to Lyndon —

INT. HALLWAY, JAMES'S FLAT — DAY

Lyndon passes a suitcase into James's waiting
hands.

Lyndon, standing in the doorway surrounded by
holdalls, bags, boxes: he's moving in.

The smiles on their faces!

Music continues over all this.

INT. BEDROOM, JAMES'S FLAT — NIGHT

Music over James and Lyndon in just their boxers on the bed, Lyndon on top of James, kissing him.

Then James pulls away.

Something's wrong.

James's confusion...

Lyndon's grin...

A small box.

Pushed down the front of Lyndon's boxers.

James's confusion...

Lyndon's grin!

Then James's hand's in there, taking out —

A jewellery box...

The surprise on James's face!

Lyndon's grin becoming a nervous smile...

James, taking it in.

Lyndon, nervous, waiting.

Waiting...

They look at each other.

Hold the stare...

Then James grins at Lyndon.

A grin that grows wider, like a door, opening —

INT. HALLWAY, JAMES AND LYNDON'S — DAY

James and Lyndon push open the front door of their new home.

Nothing special, cheap and cheerful, but it's theirs.

They step into the hallway, taking in the wallpaper, the carpets, the stairs.

Small stack of cardboard boxes, ten boxes between them, not that much to unpack.

They turn to each other and share a smile.

Lyndon holds out his hands to James.

James takes Lyndon's hands in his.

They're both wearing matching wedding rings.

Music continues over all this.

INT. BEDROOM, JAMES AND LYNDON'S — NIGHT

Music over James and Lyndon on their new bed, Lyndon on James.

Lyndon kisses James's lips.

His nose.

His eyelids.

Then Lyndon rests his forehead against James's.

And they stare into each other.

They're just about to kiss when —

They both turn to the baby monitor on the bedside table.

It's flashing.

They look back at each other.

And James sticks his tongue out at Lyndon: 'your turn'!

Lyndon sighs, nibbles the tip of James's tongue.

They swap smiles.

Then James blinks —

EXT. HIGH STREET, NORWICH CITY CENTRE — DAY

And the music ends, like a shock.

The noise of Norwich High Street at rush hour floods the scene.

And James, cute, clumsy, smiles at —

Lyndon, cool, sexy, who doesn't smile back.

Hold the stare...

Then Lyndon just walks away.

And James watches as Lyndon's carried off in the sea of shoes and suits and swinging hands.

Going...

Going...

Gone.

The disappointment on James's face...

There goes the best boyfriend he never had.

James looks down at the hand Lyndon touched.

It's still tingling...

Then James shakes it off, plugs himself into his iPod, the music he's listening to filling the scene as James walks on, slowly vanishing into the crowd.

Going...

Going...

Gone.

Hold...

Then:

Darkness.

MAN

NEW POLARI

Top. Bottom.
Sub. Dom.
Cut. Uncut.
Twink. Bear.
ASL. NSA.

It's a new polari:
the language we had to speak
when we could not speak
the love that dare not
speak its name.

DOM OR SUB?

'Are you dom or sub?'
'Domino's. I would never
eat at a Subway.'

HAIKU FOR MY TRANS FRIEND

a

broken

jigsaw

some

pieces

are

missing

you

are

in

the

wrong

box

THE WALK OF GAY SHAME

When I walk down any street, day or night,
I'm in a constant state of fight or flight,
anticipating a name calling
and anticipating a queer bashing.

Every walk is the walk of gay shame.
Every walk is like walking the plank.
Every walk: across a minefield.
Every walk: across no gay man's land.

As I walk my head talks through what I'll say
to silence someone if they shout out *gay*.
As I walk every limb is a brain
overanalysing how it's moving.

Every workman is a loaded gun.
Every pair of men's eyes are daggers.
Every passing car could throw grenades.
Every person could be a weapon.

Walking makes me as breathless as sprinting
because with each step my heart is pounding:
they are looking, laughing, jeering, sneering.
Since knowing I'm gay I've felt this feeling.

Every walk is the walk of gay shame.
Every walk is like walking the plank.
Every walk: across a minefield.
Every walk: across no gay man's land.

When I walk down any street, day or night,
I'm in a constant state of fight or flight,
anticipating a name calling
and anticipating a queer bashing.

HANDSOME HOMOPHOBES

I want you to be constantly analysing your behaviour when I'm around because you're always scared I'm going to ridicule, shame and attack how you behave.

I want you to come in my mouth and spit on my face.

I want your relationships with yourself, friends, family and partners to be forever affected by the shame I've inflicted upon you.

I want you to choke on my cock.

I want you to see me as the witty, intellectual, intelligent, articulate, romantic, cheeky, kind friend, son, uncle, brother, writer, teacher and human that I am instead of seeing me as walking sodomy.

I want you to fuck me and I want to fuck you.

I want you to stop glaring, pointing, laughing, nudging, jeering, judging and mocking.

I want you to see me and want me and want me to see you and want me to want you.

I want you to feel disgust for being a 'heterosexual man' and feel so much self-hate every time you are called those two things.

I want you to be humiliated when I tell your friends, family and girlfriend what we did in school toilets and what we do now on Snapchat when we both say we're drunk.

I want you to die the most harrowing death.

I want you to know that what you do as a homophobe is sick, sinful, ill, evil, unnatural, an abomination and against God's will.

I want you to talk to me about your relationship with your dad.

I want you to love yourself then maybe you might love me.

THE WRONG TYPE OF GAY

I went out on Saturday
to a nightclub that was gay.
Men in there stopped me to say,
Turn around and go away;
you are the wrong type of gay.

You cannot come in to play
'cause of how you mince and sway;
'cause your manner is too fey;
'cause you're such a camp cliché.
You are the wrong type of gay.

I'm the wrong type of gay, me.
I am the wrong type of gay.
I'm a minority, me,
within my minority.
I am the wrong type of gay.

Then more men joined in to say,
'Cause you can quote Doris Day;
'cause you love Bette and Mae;
'cause you sing songs from Broadway,
you are the wrong type of gay.

'Cause you don't work out all day;
'cause your pecs aren't hard as clay;
'cause your clothes are pink, not grey;
'cause you're wearing a beret...
you are the wrong type of gay.

I'm the wrong type of gay, me.
I am the wrong type of gay.
I thought it would be *we*, gee,
but it is still *them* and *me*.
I am the wrong type of gay.

LADS LADS LADS

Lads talk of tits and clits but they don't talk
of feelings; lads don't listen or smile;
lads get naked and shower together
in changing rooms; lads smash one another
in the face and on the pitch; lads are sad
and lonely; lads in gyms slap each other's
backs and bums; lads look after other lads;
lads bully lads even if they love them
as mates; lads hold each other's hands in scrums;
lads get pissed in pubs and then they have sex
with any woman; lads are uneasy
talking about their fathers; lads get scared
of being feminine; lads kill other
lads with knives and guns; lads carry coffins.

THE GYM IS LIKE A GAY BAR

The gym is like a gay bar:
men flex muscle to music
and want other men to look
and desire their body.

The gym is like a sauna:
men meet there, they undress and
they all work up a sweat, then,
when spent, shower together.

Me and them want the same thing:
the perfect male body.
But they think that it is wrong
to want what I want, and so

they invert their desire
and turn themselves into what
they want: something big and hard
that throbs with veins that pulsate.

HOOK UP

We swipe right.
Meet that night.
And we suck. And we fuck.
As we do, I love you. When it's done, my love's gone.
That was great… but it's late. Then you say, *Can I stay?*
Should say no. You should go. But those lips. And those hips
So I say, *You can stay*. And a part of my heart
prays you would stay for good. As you smoke, tell my jokes.
The patter. Then chatter. Then secrets. We connect.
Holding hands, we make plans. My heart says you will stay.
My heart prays you will stay. My head rests on your chest.
And I beam. And I dream.
Wake at dawn.
You are gone.

HOLDING HANDS

I am twenty-five and never in my life
have I held hands with a man in a public place,
just in case we come face to face
with a member of the inhuman race
who tries to debase and disgrace our gesture of love.

I am twenty-five and never in my life
have I held hands with a man in the street,
should we meet some deadbeat
who tries to defeat us and make mincemeat of us
because of our gesture of love.

I am twenty-five and never in my life
have I held hands with a man I adore
because I don't want our gesture of love to become yours.
Because our gesture of love will always be seen by you
and so our gesture of love will always be demeaned by you.

Because when two men hold hands on the pavement,
that gesture of love always becomes a political statement.
That gesture of love always becomes an event.
Because you will clock or mock, you will nudge or judge
when we just want our gesture of love to go unnoticed.

OUT AT WORK

When at work I mention that I am gay
I see your eyes become kaleidoscopes
which stop you seeing me as a human
as you start seeing me through hundreds of
little lenses of stereotypes which
have been perpetuated by culture
and cloud and confuse your judgement of me.

When I say I had drinks with my partner
you say, *We get it: you are gay, but why
do you feel the need to flaunt it?* and
you say this at your desk framed by photos
of you snogging your wife on holiday,
of your wedding day, of you and the lads
on the stag wearing 'pussy patrol' shirts.

When I tell the boss, he says, *Your being
openly gay is flaunting it to some.
Who you sleep with is a private matter
and has no place in this public workspace.*
I say, *I am not just a sex act; my
being gay affects how I see the world.*
But he's not listening as he's on Tinder.

When my partner picks me up from work, you
who always say, *Ooh, I love the gays*, wince
and flinch when you see us kiss on the lips
as my being gay is no longer just an idea;
I am no longer *just a bit camp* and
can quote Victoria Wood sketches but
really find men attractive and kiss them.

When I'm invited to a work dinner
I think on whether to bring my partner;
if my personal life is kept private
I'll seem unfriendly, but if I'm open
about my private life I may be seen

as flaunting my sexuality. So
I go alone to avoid demotion.

STRAIGHT PRIDE

Mates of mine who identify
as straight asked me to clarify
why there is no straight pride...

When are you shamed for how you identify?
When are you blamed for how you identify?
When are you nicknamed for how you identify?

Where do you face derision for how you identify?
Where are you put in prison for how you identify?
Where do you risk execution for how you identify?

That said, pride is about all of us celebrating our uniqueness.
Pride is about all of us respecting others' uniqueness.
Pride is your pride, so come and march by my side.

THE MEANING OF MARRIAGE

Marriage is a union between a man and a woman.
To you, maybe, but not to me.
To me marriage is a union between a human and a human.

But marriage means a union between a man and a woman.
To you, maybe, but not to me.
I don't use your dictionary.
Just as we all define love differently
we all define marriage differently.
And, you see, old words change their meaning
when new ideas change the world they're describing.

No. Marriage means a union between a man and a woman.
To you, maybe, but not to me.
To me marriage isn't a semantic issue;
to me marriage is a romantic issue
between two people.
Two.
And, unless one of those is you,
I don't see why you'd have a view
on what those two people do
as their love doesn't directly affect you.

My faith defines marriage as a union between a man and a woman.
I respect your faith, but don't impose it onto me,
because I've got faith in something else, you see:
I've got faith in equality
and in my faith we define marriage differently.

You marrying a man lessens my marriage to a woman.
To you, maybe, but not to me.
Because that's nonsensical to me.
When I marry, nothing's taken from you and given to me.
When I marry, my marrying doesn't rewrite your history.

I think men like you dislike men like me who marry
as you secretly envy why we marry:

we don't get married just because our parents did;
we don't get married just because we want to parent kids;
we get married just because we love who we're with.

I think men like you like to dislike men like me who marry
to make you feel better about your marriage that's unhappy,
and maybe it's unhappy as you were told who to marry
by family, by society, by Christianity,
and so I think deep down you see
why it really gets to me
when some stranger tells me
who I can marry.

SO LONG, SOHO

So long, Soho.
You boozy floozy.
You pretty shitty witty fitty.
You liver of London.
You giver of freedom.
You sliver of individuality in this drain of chains we call a city.
You are withering because suited vultures mad for money
are selling off your solace for many
to build houses, offices and crap-coffee-selling orifices for the
few
and there is nothing we can do.

So long, Soho.
So long to your gay pubs
and drag clubs
and art hubs
where smart cubs dreamt up ways to better our culture.
Because suited vultures mad for money
are turning your once-sacred gay ground
into an investor's playground
and they're uprooting you and me.

So long, Soho.
Where now do the bohos, hobos and homos who made this
home go?
Where now do the queers, queens, has-beens and never-beens
avoid life's meanness?
Can we not have one place that is ours
without you having to build towers on it?
So.
So long, Soho.
So long.

PROMISCUOUS ANXIOUS ALCOHOLICS

Some of us are promiscuous.
But you can't blame us.
Since birth you've told us
gay men are not monogamous
and love cannot exist between us.
Plus… some of us just love penis
and want to play and lay with many partners
before we say for sure which one stays with us,
not because we're homosexual
but because we're *Homo sapiens*
and that's usually how humans find who they love.

Some of us are big drinkers.
But you can't blame us.
We're just drowning out your wicked whispers
and we can't meet a man in the streets like you can.
We can't hold hands in the streets like you can
or we run the risk of violence from some caveman.
The only safe spaces we can find connection with people like
us,
the only safe spaces we can show affection to people like us,
the only safe spaces we don't face derision simply for being us
are in gay pubs and clubs
and that is why we have to learn to like the liquor.
Plus… some of us just like getting plastered
and drunk dancing along to the songs of ABBA,
not because we're homosexual
but because we're *Homo sapiens*
and humans like to get pissed and get their groove on.

Some of us are anxious.
But you can't blame us.
Since birth you've told us,
you covert cultural child abusers,
that we are sinners simply for being us.
As tots, then teens, we spent ages
trying to hide telltale queeny gestures

and dampen and stamp out our camp voices
as everyday strangers were shaming us.
Everyday strangers were naming us.
Everyday strangers were claiming us to be monsters.
Plus… we aren't anxious because we're homosexual.
We're anxious because we're *Homo sapiens*.
We're all raw, unsure and insecure
on this rock that's racked with war
wondering what life is for.

So yes: some of us are promiscuous, big drinkers and anxious.
But you can't blame us;
we just behave like this because of how you shame us.

FOURTEEN THINGS I WISH I COULD TELL MY FOURTEEN-YEAR-OLD SELF

Don't wait until you're eighteen to start living openly as a gay man. You and everyone who matters to you already knows that you're gay and they will be fine with it. Because you don't come out until you're eighteen, there are so many boys you never kiss or sleep with who wanted to kiss or sleep with you. You will regularly regret not kissing or sleeping with them.

You'll be a professional writer, performer and creative writing teacher. Your dreams come true.

Don't waste time on relationships with people solely because they're sexy, popular or well-connected in the arts. They will leave you feeling fake, inferior or bored. Time spent with them could be time spent singing with Mum, laughing with Amber or talking with Lyndon.

Don't try to be cool. Don't try to be hot. Don't try to be cold. Just be warm. You don't have to try to be warm.

Do not get social media. You will get addicted to getting likes, your attention span will get fucked and you'll get sad because you'll compare your life to the lies other people tell online about their lives. The time you spend on social media shouting about having experiences could be time spent having experiences.

You will be funny, chatty, clever, kind, creative, trusted and respected. You will wear great blazers, you will have a great beard and you will have a great quiff.

Dad adores you. He just doesn't understand you yet. Because you don't understand you yet. And so you can't show Dad who you are yet. But you'll come to understand who you are, you'll show Dad, he'll understand you and he'll love you for being you.

No one really cares about how you look or who you sleep with because they're too busy caring about how they look and who they sleep with, so stop worrying about how you look and who you sleep with and just look how you like and sleep with who you want.

Gay men don't just have sexual relationships with each other. You will have profound friendships with so many gay men. You will console each other about your pasts and help each other through your presents. You will teach each other things school should have taught you: how to love yourselves, how to love each other and what your history is.

You will be all right at sex, you will be kissed loads and you will get a job you love, so stop wasting childhood worrying about adulthood because as an adult you will mourn the fact you spent childhood worrying about being an adult.

You will meet Stephen Fry; he will hug you and tell you that he likes your bow tie.

Don't wear bow ties.

Don't wait until you're eighteen before you start listening to Morrissey. His music is medicine.

It will all be all right, Jimmy Mac. Be brave enough to be yourself and live your truth. I love you. Because you've been shamed, you don't love you yet. But you will. You will. You will.

EPILOGUE

GRINDR PROFILE 2020

James, 26

Online now

Hello. I'm a writer and creative writing teacher. I love writing, reading, walking, laughing and deep chats. I'm not mad about the beard either but without it I look like Clare Balding so…

Height: 178cm

Weight: 9st 10lb

Body Type: Average

Position: Versatile Bottom

Ethnicity: White

Relationship Status: Single

My Tribes: Geek, Rugged, Twink

Looking For: Dates, Friends, Relationships, Right Now

Gender: Cis Man

Pronouns: He/Him/His

HIV Status: Negative

ACKNOWLEDGEMENTS

My thanks to all the friends, family members and fellas who inspired the poems in *Manatomy*.

My thanks to Bridget Hart, Clive Birnie, Harriet Evans and everyone at Burning Eye Books for editing, designing and publishing *Manatomy*.

My thanks to Stephen Fry, Luke Wright, Molly Naylor, Jonathan Harvey, David McAlmont and Ian Giles for their quotes on *Manatomy*.

My thanks to Lucy Farrant and Pasco Q Kevlin for hosting the Norfolk book launch of *Manatomy* at Norwich Arts Centre and for producing the accompanying book tour.

My thanks to Ian Giles, Kaavous Clayton and everyone at originalprojects for commissioning me to write 'Straight Pride' for Open Ramble East: Colchester 2019.

My thanks to Marcus Romer, Simon Poulter and everyone at Luton Art & Culture for commissioning me to write 'The Walk of Gay Shame' and 'Teaching Kids About Gay Relationships' for People Power Passion: Justice 39.

My thanks to my agents Jessi Stewart and Anwar Chentoufi at Independent Talent for looking after me.

My thanks to the staff of Wells Deli Holt for providing me with company and coffee during the rewriting of *Manatomy*.

My thanks to Rachel Connor for giving me that copy of Rupert Everett's autobiography which made me come out and write.

My thanks to my best mates Mark, Cam, Rob, Jake, Lyndon, Charlie, Nick and Amber for being there and for being them.

And my thanks to Mum and Dad. Nature or nurture: either way, you are responsible for all of this and I couldn't be more grateful.

Lightning Source UK Ltd.
Milton Keynes UK
UKHW010418050821
388320UK00002B/257